THE UPPER ROOM
Book of Christmas Carols
REVISED EDITION

THE UPPER ROOM® BOOK OF CHRISTMAS CAROLS
Revised Edition
Copyright © 2004 Upper Room Ministries®
All rights reserved.

No part of this work may be reproduced or transmitted in any form or by any means, electronic or mechanical, including photocopying and recording, or by any information storage or retrieval system, except as may be expressly permitted by the 1976 Copyright Act or in writing from the publisher. For information, write Upper Room Books, 1908 Grand Avenue, Nashville, TN 37212.

Upper Room Books® website: upperroombooks.com

Upper Room Ministries®, Upper Room Books®, and design logos are trademarks owned by The Upper Room®, Nashville, Tennessee. All rights reserved.

We are grateful to Dean McIntyre, director of music resources in the Center for Worship Resourcing, General Board of Discipleship, for his consultation and guidance on this project.

Scripture is from the New Revised Standard Version Bible, copyright © 1989, Division of Christian Education of the National Council of the Churches of Christ in the United States of America. Used by permission. All rights reserved.

The first prayer on page 5 is from The Book of Common Prayer (New York: The Church Hymnal Corporation and The Seabury Press, 1977), 212.

NOTE TO ACCOMPANISTS: Brackets indicate suggested introductions for each song.

Cover image: © PhotoDisc
Music typesetting: Don Schlosser

ISBN 978-0-8358-1946-6

Contents

Carol Service	5
Angels from the Realms of Glory	7
Angels We Have Heard on High	8
Away in a Manger	9
Bring a Torch, Jeannette, Isabella	10
Deck the Halls	11
Gentle Mary Laid Her Child	12
God Rest You Merry, Gentlemen	13
Good Christian Friends, Rejoice	14
Go, Tell It on the Mountain	15
Hark! The Herald Angels Sing	16
He Is Born (*Il Est Né*)	17
How Great Our Joy	18
I Heard the Bells on Christmas Day	19
It Came upon the Midnight Clear	20
Joseph Dearest, Joseph Mine	21
Joy to the World! The Lord Is Come	22
O Come, All Ye Faithful	23
O Come, Little Children	24
O Come, O Come, Emmanuel	25
O Little Town of Bethlehem	26
Once in Royal David's City	27
Rise Up, Shepherd, and Follow	28
Silent Night, Holy Night	29
Sing We Now of Christmas	30
The First Noel	31
The Virgin Mary Had a Baby Boy	32
We Three Kings	34
We Wish You a Merry Christmas	35
What Child Is This?	36

Carol Service

In the following service, vary the singing by using solo voices, singing stanzas in unison, and alternating between men and women. *The Upper Room* daily devotional guide is a good source for meditations.

SCRIPTURE: "God so loved the world that he gave his only Son, so that everyone who believes in him may not perish but may have eternal life" (John 3:16).

PRAYER: O God, you make us glad by the yearly festival of the birth of your only Son Jesus Christ: Grant that we, who joyfully receive him as our Redeemer, may with sure confidence behold him when he comes to be our Judge; who lives and reigns with you and the Holy Spirit, one God, now and forever. Amen.

CAROLS: "O Come, All Ye Faithful" (page 23); "God Rest You Merry, Gentlemen" (page 13)

THE HOLY FAMILY IN BETHLEHEM: Read Luke 2:1-7.

CAROLS: "O Little Town of Bethlehem" (page 26); "Gentle Mary Laid Her Child" (page 12); "Silent Night, Holy Night" (page 29)

SHEPHERDS HEAR OF THE BIRTH OF CHRIST: Read Luke 2:8-20.

CAROLS: "The First Noel" (page 31); "Rise Up, Shepherd, and Follow" (page 28); "Angels We Have Heard on High" (page 8)

WISE MEN SEEK THE CHILD: Read Matthew 2:1-12.

CAROLS: "We Three Kings" (page 34); "Sing We Now of Christmas" (page 30)

MEDITATION

CAROLS: "Go, Tell It on the Mountain" (page 15); "Joy to the World! The Lord Is Come" (page 22)

PRAYER: Eternal God, we are thankful you have given yourself to humankind by the birth of your Son, Jesus Christ. We pray that many hearts the world over may search for and find him. In Christ's name we pray. Amen.

Angels from the Realms of Glory

1. Angels from the realms of glory, Wing your flight o'er all the earth; Ye who sang creation's story Now proclaim Messiah's birth: Come and worship, come and worship, Worship Christ, the new-born King.
2. Shepherds in the field abiding, Watching o'er your flocks by night, God with us is now residing; Yonder shines the infant light: Come and worship, come and worship, Worship Christ, the new-born King.
3. Sages, leave your contemplations, Brighter visions beam afar; Seek the great Desire of nations; Ye have seen his natal star: Come and worship, come and worship, Worship Christ, the new-born King.
4. Saints, before the altar bending, Watching long in hope and fear; Suddenly the Lord, descending, In his temple shall appear: Come and worship, come and worship, Worship Christ, the new-born King.

WORDS: James Montgomery, 1771–1854, alt.
MUSIC: Henry T. Smart, 1813–1879

Angels We Have Heard on High

WORDS: Traditional French carol; trans. *Crown of Jesus*, 1862, alt.
MUSIC: Traditional French carol; arr. by Edward Shippen Barnes, 1887–1958

Away in a Manger

1. Away in a manger, no crib for a bed, The little Lord Jesus laid down his sweet head; The stars in the sky looked down where he lay, The little Lord Jesus, asleep on the hay.

2. The cattle are lowing, the Baby awakes, But little Lord Jesus, no crying he makes; I love thee, Lord Jesus! look down from the sky, And stay by my cradle till morning is nigh.

3. Be near me, Lord Jesus, I ask thee to stay Close by me forever, and love me, I pray; Bless all the dear children in thy tender care, And fit us for heaven to live with thee there.

WORDS: St. 1, 2, anonymous, 1885; st. 3, John Thomas McFarland, 1851–1913
MUSIC: James R. Murray, 1841–1905

Bring a Torch, Jeannette, Isabella

WORDS: Traditional French carol
MUSIC: Traditional French carol

Deck the Halls

1. Deck the halls with boughs of hol-ly, Fa la la la la, la la la la.
'Tis the sea-son to be jol-ly, Fa la la la la, la la la la.
Don we now our gay ap-par-el, Fa la la la la la, la la la.
Troll the an-cient yule-tide car-ol, Fa la la la la, la la la la.

2. See the blaz-ing yule be-fore us, Fa la la la la, la la la la.
Strike the harp and join the cho-rus, Fa la la la la, la la la la.
Fol-low me in mer-ry meas-ure, Fa la la la la la, la la la la.
While I tell of yule-tide treas-ure, Fa la la la la, la la la la.

3. Fast a-way the old year pass-es,
Hail the new, ye lads and lass-es,
Sing we joy-ous all to-geth-er,
Heed-less of the wind and weath-er,

WORDS: Traditional Welsh carol, alt.
MUSIC: Traditional Welsh melody

Gentle Mary Laid Her Child

1. Gentle Mary laid her Child Lowly in a manger;
   There he lay, the undefiled, To the world a stranger.
   Such a Babe in such a place, Can he be the Savior?
   Ask the saved of all the race Who have found his favor.

2. Angels sang about his birth; Wise Men sought and found him;
   Heaven's star shone brightly forth, Glory all around him.
   Shepherds saw the wondrous sight, Heard the angels singing;
   All the plains were lit that night, All the hills were ringing.

3. Gentle Mary laid her Child Lowly in a manger;
   He is still the undefiled, But no more a stranger.
   Son of God, of humble birth, Beautiful the story;
   Praise his name in all the earth, Hail the King of glory.

WORDS: Joseph S. Cook, 1859–1933
MUSIC: 14th-century spring carol; arr. by Ernest MacMillan, 1893–1973

God Rest You Merry, Gentlemen

1. God rest you merry, gentlemen,* Let nothing you dismay,
   Remember Christ our Savior Was born on Christmas Day,
   To save us all from Satan's pow'r When we were gone astray.
   O tidings of comfort and joy, comfort and joy; O tidings of comfort and joy.

2. From God, our heav'nly Father, A blessed angel came;
   And unto certain shepherds Brought tidings of the same:
   How that in Bethlehem was born The Son of God by name.

3. "Fear not," then said the angel, "Let nothing you affright;
   This day is born a Savior Of a pure virgin bright,
   To free all those who trust in him From Satan's pow'r and might."

4. Now to the Lord sing praises, All you within this place,
   And with true love and fellowship Each other now embrace;
   This holy tide of Christmas All others doth efface.

*Substitute *gentle folk* for *gentlemen*, if desired.
WORDS: 18th-century English carol, alt.
MUSIC: Traditional English carol; arr. John Stainer, 1840–1901

Good Christian Friends, Rejoice

WORDS: 14th-century Latin carol; trans. by John Mason Neale, 1818–1866, alt.
MUSIC: Traditional German melody, 14th century; harm. adapted from John Stainer, 1840–1901

Go, Tell It on the Mountain

WORDS: John J. Work Jr., 1872–1925
MUSIC: African American spiritual; arr. Don Schlosser, 1956–
Arr. © 2004 Upper Room Ministries

He Is Born
(Il Est Né)

WORDS: Traditional French carol, 19th century
MUSIC: Traditional French carol, 18th century; harm. by Don Schlosser, 1956–
Harm. © 2004 Upper Room Ministries

I Heard the Bells on Christmas Day

*Substitute *all* for *men*, if desired.
WORDS: Henry W. Longfellow, 1807–1882
MUSIC: John Calkin, 1827–1905

Joseph Dearest, Joseph Mine

WORDS: Traditional German carol; trans. by Percy Dearmer, 1867–1936
MUSIC: Traditional German carol

Joy to the World! The Lord Is Come

WORDS: Isaac Watts, 1674–1748
MUSIC: Attributed to George F. Handel, 1685–1759; arr. attributed to Lowell Mason, 1792–1872

O Come, All Ye Faithful
(Adeste Fideles)

WORDS: Latin hymn; ascribed to John F. Wade, c. 1710–1786;
          trans. by Frederick Oakeley, 1802–1880, and others
MUSIC: John F. Wade, c. 1710–1786

O Come, Little Children

1. O come, little children, o come, one and all,
To Bethlehem's stable, in Bethlehem's stall,
And see with rejoicing this glorious sight,
Our Father in heaven has sent us this night.

2. O see in the manger, in hallowed light
A star throws its beam on this holiest sight.
In clean swaddling clothes lies the heavenly Child,
More lovely than angels, this Baby so mild.

3. Oh, there lies the Christ child, on hay and on straw;
The shepherds are kneeling before him with awe.
And Mary and Joseph smile on him with love,
While angels are singing sweet songs from above.

WORDS: Johann A. P. Schulz, 1747–1800
MUSIC: Johann A. P. Schulz, 1747–1800

O Come, O Come, Emmanuel

WORDS: Latin hymn; trans. by John M. Neale, 1818–1866
MUSIC: 13th-century plainsong; arr. and harm. by Thomas Helmore, 1811–1890

O Little Town of Bethlehem

WORDS: Phillips Brooks, 1835–1893
MUSIC: Lewis H. Redner, 1831–1908

Once in Royal David's City

WORDS: Cecil Frances Alexander, 1823–1895
MUSIC: Henry J. Gauntlett, 1805–1976

Rise Up, Shepherd, and Follow

1. There's a star in the east on Christ-mas morn;
2. If you take good heed to the an-gel's words;

Rise up, shep-herd and fol-low; It will lead to the place where the
Rise up, shep-herd, and fol-low; You'll for-get your flocks, you'll for-

Christ is born; Rise up, shep-herd, and fol-low.
get your herds; Rise up, shep-herd, and fol-low.

Refrain
Fol-low, fol-low, rise up, shep-herd, and fol-low, fol-low the star of Beth-le-hem. Rise up, shep-herd, and fol-low.

WORDS: African American spiritual
MUSIC: African American spiritual

Silent Night, Holy Night

WORDS: Joseph Mohr, 1792–1849; trans. compiled from various sources
MUSIC: Franz Gruber, 1787–1863

Sing We Now of Christmas

1. Sing we now of Christ-mas, No-el, sing we here!
2. An-gels called to shep-herds, "Leave your flocks at rest;
3. In the stall they found him; Jo-seph and Ma-ry mild
4. From the east-ern coun-try came the kings a-far,
5. Gold and myrrh they took there, gifts of great-est price;

Hear our grate-ful prais-es to the Babe so dear.
Jour-ney forth to Beth-l'hem, find the Child so blest."
Seat-ed by the man-ger, watch-ing the ho-ly Child.
Bear-ing gifts to Beth-l'hem, guid-ed by a star.
There was ne'er a sta-ble so like par-a-dise.

Sing we No-el, the King is born, No-el!

Sing we now of Christ-mas, sing we now No-el!

WORDS: Traditional French carol
MUSIC: Traditional French carol; arr. by Don Schlosser, 1956–
Arr. © 2004 Upper Room Ministries

The First Noel

WORDS: Traditional English carol, alt.
MUSIC: Traditional English carol; harm. from *Christmas Carols New and Old*, 1871

The Virgin Mary Had a Baby Boy

WORDS: Traditional West Indian carol
MUSIC: West Indian carol; arr. by Don Schlosser, 1956–
Arr. © 2004 Upper Room Ministries

We Wish You a Merry Christmas

WORDS: Traditional English carol
MUSIC: Traditional English carol; arr. by Don Schlosser, 1956–
Arr. © 2004 Upper Room Ministries

CPSIA information can be obtained
at www.ICGtesting.com
Printed in the USA
JSHW040607160922
30574JS00002B/11